Copyright © 2020 June Day

WHO?

WHY?

HOW?

PEOPLE I Want to SLAP

WHO?

WHY?

HOW?

WHO?

WHY?

HOW?

WHO?

WHY?

HOW?

WHO?

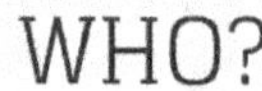

WHY?

HOW?

PEOPLE I Want to SLAP

WHO?

WHY?

HOW?

WHO?

WHY?

HOW?

PEOPLE I Want to SLAP

WHO?

WHY?

HOW?

WHO?

WHY?

HOW?

PEOPLE I Want to SLAP

WHY?

HOW?

WHO?

WHY?

HOW?

PEOPLE I Want to SLAP

WHO?

WHY?

HOW?

WHO?

WHY?

HOW?

WHO?

WHY?

HOW?

WHO?

WHY?

HOW?

PEOPLE I Want to SLAP

WHO?

WHY?

HOW?

WHO?

WHY?

HOW?

PEOPLE I Want to SLAP

WHO?

WHY?

HOW?

WHO?

WHY?

HOW?

PEOPLE I want to SLAP

WHO?

WHY?

HOW?

PEOPLE I Want to SLAP

WHO?

WHY?

HOW?

PEOPLE I Want to SLAP

WHO?

WHY?

HOW?

WHO?

WHY?

HOW?

PEOPLE I Want to SLAP

WHO?

WHY?

HOW?

WHO?

WHY?

HOW?

PEOPLE I Want to SLAP

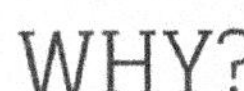

WHO?

WHY?

HOW?

WHO?

WHY?

HOW?

WHY?

HOW?

WHO?

WHY?

HOW?

WHY?

HOW?

WHO?

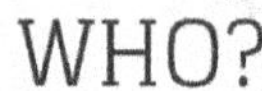

WHY?

HOW?

PEOPLE I Want to SLAP

WHO?

WHY?

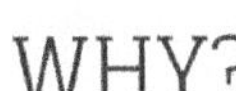

HOW?

WHO?

WHY?

HOW?

WHO?

WHY?

HOW?

WHO?

WHY?

HOW?

WHO?

WHY?

HOW?

WHO?

WHY?

HOW?

PEOPLE I want to SLAP

WHO?

WHY?

HOW?

WHO?

WHY?

HOW?

PEOPLE I Want to SLAP

WHO?

WHY?

HOW?

WHO?

WHY?

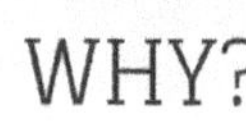

HOW?

PEOPLE I want to SLAP

WHO?

WHY?

HOW?

WHO?

WHY?

HOW?

PEOPLE I Want to SLAP

WHO?

WHY?

HOW?

WHO?

WHY?

HOW?

WHO?

WHY?

HOW?

WHO?

WHY?

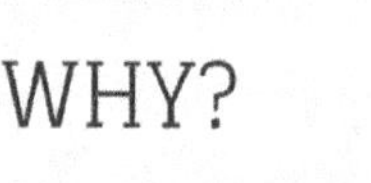

HOW?

PEOPLE I Want to SLAP

WHY?

WHO?

HOW?

WHO?

WHY?

HOW?

PEOPLE I Want to SLAP

WHO?

WHY?

HOW?

WHO?

WHY?

HOW?

PEOPLE I Want to SLAP

WHO?

WHY?

HOW?

WHO?

WHY?

HOW?

PEOPLE I Want to SLAP

WHO?

WHY?

HOW?

WHO?

WHY?

HOW?

PEOPLE I Want to SLAP

WHO?

WHY?

HOW?

WHO?

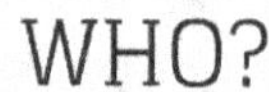

WHY?

HOW?

PEOPLE I Want to SLAP

WHO?

WHY?

HOW?

WHO?

WHY?

HOW?

WHO?

WHY?

HOW?

WHO?

WHY?

HOW?

PEOPLE I Want to SLAP

WHO?

WHY?

HOW?

WHO?

WHY?

HOW?

PEOPLE I Want to SLAP

WHO?

WHY?

HOW?

WHO?

WHY?

HOW?

WHO?

WHY?

HOW?

WHO?

WHY?

HOW?

WHO?

WHY?

HOW?

PEOPLE I Want to SLAP

WHO?

WHY?

HOW?

PEOPLE I Want to SLAP

WHO?

WHY?

HOW?

WHO?

WHY?

HOW?

WHO?

WHY?

HOW?

WHO?

WHY?

HOW?

WHO?

WHY?

HOW?

WHO?

WHY?

HOW?

WHO?

WHY?

HOW?

WHO?

WHY?

HOW?

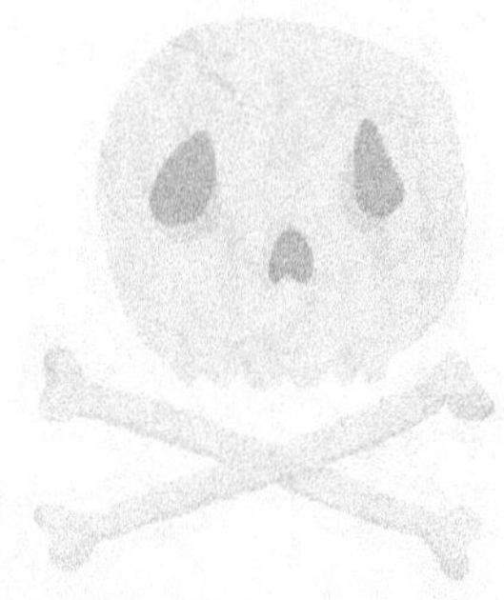

WHO?

WHY?

HOW?

WHO?

WHY?

HOW?

WHO?

WHY?

HOW?

WHO?

WHY?

HOW?

WHO?

WHY?

HOW?

WHO?

WHY?

HOW?

WHO?

WHY?

HOW?

WHO?

WHY?

HOW?

WHY?

HOW?

WHO?

WHY?

HOW?

PEOPLE
I
Want
to
SLAP

WHO?

WHY?

HOW?

WHY?

HOW?

PEOPLE I Want to SLAP

WHO?

WHY?

HOW?

WHO?

WHY?

HOW?

PEOPLE I Want to SLAP

WHY?

WHO?

HOW?

WHO?

WHY?

HOW?

PEOPLE I Want to SLAP

WHO?

WHY?

HOW?

WHO?

WHY?

HOW?

WHO?

WHY?

HOW?

WHO?

WHY?

HOW?

PEOPLE I Want to SLAP

WHO?

WHY?

HOW?

WHO?

WHY?

HOW?

PEOPLE I Want to SLAP

WHO?

WHY?

HOW?

WHO?

WHY?

HOW?

WHO?

WHY?

HOW?

WHO?

WHY?

HOW?

WHO?

WHY?

HOW?

WHO?

WHY?

HOW?

WHO?

WHY?

HOW?

WHO?

WHY?

HOW?

PEOPLE I Want to SLAP

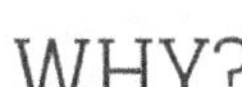

WHY?

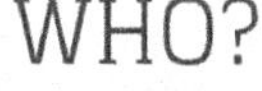

WHO?

HOW?

WHO?

WHY?

HOW?

WHO?

WHY?

HOW?

WHO?

WHY?

HOW?

WHO?

WHY?

HOW?

WHO?

WHY?

HOW?

WHO?

WHY?

HOW?

WHO?

WHY?

HOW?

WHO?

WHY?

HOW?

WHO?

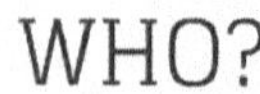

WHY?

HOW?

WHO?

WHY?

HOW?

WHO?

WHY?

HOW?